Broken but Blessed

Broken but Blessed

*Journeying from Pain to Peace
with Unlikely Guides*

Rebekah Domer

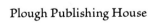

Plough Publishing House

Published by Plough Publishing House
Walden, New York
Robertsbridge, England
Elsmore, Australia
www.plough.com

Plough produces books, a quarterly magazine, and Plough.com to encourage people and help them put their faith into action. We believe Jesus can transform the world and that his teachings and example apply to all aspects of life. At the same time, we seek common ground with all people regardless of their creed.

Plough is the publishing house of the Bruderhof, an international community of families and singles seeking to follow Jesus together. Members of the Bruderhof are committed to a way of radical discipleship in the spirit of the Sermon on the Mount. Inspired by the first church in Jerusalem (Acts 2 and 4), they renounce private property and share everything in common in a life of nonviolence, justice, and service to neighbors near and far. To learn more about the Bruderhof's faith, history, and daily life, see Bruderhof. com. (Views expressed by Plough authors are their own and do not necessarily reflect the position of the Bruderhof.)

ISBN: 978-0-87486-763-3
Copyright © 2018 by Plough Publishing House
All rights reserved.

A catalog record for this book is available from the British Library.
Library of Congress Cataloging-in-Publication Data
Names: Domer, Rebekah, author.
Title: Broken but blessed : journeying from pain to peace with unlikely
guides / Rebekah Domer.
Description: Walden : Plough Publishing House, 2018.
Identifiers: LCCN 2018006811 | ISBN 9780874867633
Subjects: LCSH: Beatitudes--Criticism, interpretation, etc. |
Suffering--Religious aspects--Christianity. | Consolation.
Classification: LCC BT382 .D628 2018 | DDC 241.5/3--dc23 LC record
available at https://lccn.loc.gov/2018006811

Contents

Foreword vii

Introduction xi

1 The Poor in Spirit 1

2 Those Who Mourn 17

3 The Meek 29

4 Those Who Hunger 43

5 The Merciful 59

6 The Pure in Heart 73

7 The Peacemakers 89

8 The Persecuted 103

Postscript 119

Foreword

W HEN I WAS in hospital with a broken hip several years ago, Father Benedict Groeschel, CFR, came to visit me. He said, "Alice, don't waste your suffering." I have meditated on that ever since, because suffering is meant to transform you and bring you closer to Christ.

Don't get me wrong: to be crippled, as I am now, is horrible. But to see how people care for me reminds me of God's goodness, and that gives me joy and gratitude. If you don't look at life through the eyes of faith, everything is rain and darkness and fog. But once you have the eyes of faith, you see.

This book, *Broken but Blessed,* is rooted in the Beatitudes, which are so desperately needed today. The Beatitudes are beautiful precisely because in them Jesus lifts up the poor and the weak and the helpless. He totally upends the world's understanding of what brings happiness.

Kierkegaard has said it's only on our knees that we can understand the Bible. This is exactly what modern people don't want to do. As G. K. Chesterton writes, "Modern man forgets how tall he is on his knees." How beautifully said! How tall we are on our knees – and how small when we are on stilts – because the truth can only be perceived by the humble.

So before you read the Beatitudes, go on your knees and say, "Give me the grace to understand them properly." Then read them on your knees, figuratively, as a hungry beggar, knowing that this is divine food. If you persevere, the Beatitudes will become your daily food.

We have each been wounded, sometimes very badly. All of us have faults and have made mistakes. But God has not completely abandoned us. We may be sick, but we are not totally helpless. The first step to the happiness that Jesus promises we must take ourselves: we must accept our weakness, our imperfections, our spiritual poverty. To do this requires one of the most crucial virtues of the Gospel: humility. And who teaches us humility? Christ, who became a man to share our weak human nature. He knew suffering. He knew anguish. He knew fear.

This is why Jesus' Beatitudes are such an unbelievable gift. When we discover our weakness, we turn to God for help. We don't deny our helplessness but say to God, "You can do it." And he does.

Whatever happens to you, know that there is a God who has created you and loves you and wants the best for you. Whatever happens, simply say, "My God, it might not have been my choice, but it is your choice, and therefore I accept it." If you can do this, I am convinced that, like the amazing people Rebekah Domer has profiled in this book, you too will find the peace that the Beatitudes offer.

Alice von Hildebrand
New Rochelle, NY
January 2018

Introduction

"WHY ME?" IS THE CRY I hear most often in my work as a hospice chaplain. Most of us, I imagine, have flung this anguished question heavenward in an hour of despair. Suffering is an enigma, a theme that emerges repeatedly in my encounters with patients, their families, and even the staff who diligently care for them.

I've got questions enough myself. But I hold on to the assurance that God is with us, regardless of circumstances. His wisdom surpasses our comprehension, and he is weaving a masterpiece in which every life contributes a distinct hue. My own experiences, and what others have shared with me, validate thoughts of Grant Colfax Tullar in his well-known poem, "The Weaver."

> . . . The dark threads are as needful
> In the weaver's skillful hand

As the threads of gold and silver
In the pattern He has planned.

He knows, He loves, He cares;
Nothing this truth can dim.
He gives the very best to those
Who chose to walk with Him.

Throughout history people have wrestled with suffering.
Would a loving God stand aloof, not lifting a finger to
right the world's wrongs? We may not understand much
of what life brings our way. But I believe God has a plan
for every soul, a unique pathway intended to lead to
peace. He has not abandoned us, as it may sometimes
seem. He sent an envoy of love, who became one of us.
Jesus walked the countercultural road to peace and
showed us the way to live.

In *Prayer and the Quest for Healing,* Barbara Fiand
says, "The strong and ruthless among us will be brought
low," and goes on to explain that "they will encounter
personal vulnerability and sin and will in due time be
invited to surrender in order to become whole."

I'm not a theologian or Bible scholar, but through my
encounters with people who are elderly, disabled, dying,
and bereaved – and through my own quest for peace – a
particular component of Jesus' teaching known as the

Beatitudes (Matt. 5:1–8) has become essential. These blessings were spoken to the crowds on a grassy hill in Judea long ago. More than a historical speech, however, they describe the attributes of God's people. According to the Beatitudes, it is the humble who will inherit his kingdom. Beaten down by life, their suffering has honed them, divesting them of pride and opening them to new vistas of righteousness. Whether you consider yourself a Christian or not, you too can be encouraged by Jesus' Beatitudes:

> Blessed are the poor in spirit, for theirs is the kingdom of heaven.
> Blessed are they who mourn, for they shall be comforted.
> Blessed are the meek, for they shall inherit the earth.
> Blessed are they who hunger and thirst for righteousness, for they shall be satisfied.
> Blessed are the merciful, for they shall obtain mercy.
> Blessed are the pure in heart, for they shall see God.
> Blessed are the peacemakers, for they shall be called children of God.
> Blessed are they who are persecuted for the sake of righteousness, for theirs is the kingdom of heaven.

Broken but Blessed is a journey through the lives of ordinary folk. Perhaps you, like one of them, are up against insurmountable odds, battling illness, or devastated by loss. You may have been rejected, betrayed, or abused. Whatever you are facing, these people who have walked life's valleys can accompany you through your own valley toward the blessings that the Beatitudes promise us.

1

The Poor in Spirit

Blessed are the poor in spirit,
for theirs is the kingdom of heaven.

My Story

In Love's service, only wounded soldiers can serve.

Thornton Wilder

FOR TWENTY-EIGHT YEARS I was cruising. Life was great, opportunities endless. I was energetic and healthy. Teaching children both contributed to my community and brought me fulfillment.

And then I crashed.

I was teaching four- and five-year-olds that afternoon. I still remember how the late-summer sun was shimmering through the trees as I stood up to serve snack. I gasped. Searing pain was shooting down my leg. Putting on a brave front, I made it through the afternoon, but by evening I could barely walk.

I tried to shrug off my pain as a passing annoyance, but my situation deteriorated. Next morning saw me face up on a cold steel table as a CT scanner registered cross-sectional images of my lower back. I was summoned to my doctor's office and told I had a degenerative condition of the spine that would change the course of my life forever.

Refusing to accept the diagnosis, I signed on for a year as a nanny with a family in New York City – a challenging assignment at best. But three weeks into the job, I found myself stranded at a bookstore, my four-year-old charge in tow. My troublesome leg was suddenly, without warning, totally paralyzed.

Emergency surgery followed, then weeks of recuperation, but I've never been the same. Pain has become my constant companion, sapping my strength and preventing sleep. Where previously nothing was too much, I now had to push through a wall of enervating weakness to perform the smallest task.

Resigning myself to permanent disability at the age of twenty-eight seemed pointless. "Why?" was my angry demand. Was God punishing me? Had I been remiss in serving him? Why else would he slam life's doors on me? I could no longer contribute – I was nothing but a burden! Hurt, ashamed, and conflicted, I sought solace in a nearby convent.

"I don't understand!" I cried to Sister Agnes, the convent's superior, as I sat in her office. "If God wants me to serve him, why has he robbed me of my capabilities?"

She looked at me, her eyes clear and direct. The love in her voice calmed my anger as she asked, "Rebekah, have you ever read the Beatitudes?"

The Beatitudes? Of *course* I had read the Beatitudes! These virtues Jesus articulated are central to my faith. But what did they have to do with my current situation?

"Read the first Beatitude, Rebekah," Sister Agnes said quietly. "It holds the answer for you. Your pain can be a *gift* if it teaches you humility."

I was silent as she pressed on. "Don't you see God's wisdom in stopping you in your tracks? He desires *you,* Rebekah. Not great achievements or valiant efforts; He wants *you.*"

"Just *be.* Simply offer him your love and allow yourself to *be* loved. That is all he asks!"

This was new terrain for me. I went home and read the first Beatitude again, "Blessed are the poor in spirit, for theirs is the kingdom of heaven." Jesus was offering me poverty of spirit, and I was rebelling.

Everyone on this planet suffers. Sooner or later, we'll all be broken in the business of living. At such times we may wonder if God is punishing or even mocking us. Years have passed since that October day in Sister Agnes's office – years in which I have pondered the Beatitudes repeatedly. Life has been tough, my faith tested. But I am learning to trust God.

And I have discovered that Sister Agnes was right. Jesus' love, as expressed in the Beatitudes, was the key that could unlock the muddled recesses of my soul and guide me from "achievement" toward poverty of spirit.

Louisa

*The kingdom of heaven is theirs already; they are
already looking at the world as God sees it,
and their values are God's values.*

Gerald O'Mahony

W<small>HENEVER I READ</small> the first Beatitude, I think of
my sister Louisa. Almost two years older than I, Louisa
was born with Down syndrome and an inoperable heart
defect. Back then, people with developmental disabilities
were usually institutionalized and denied education
and advanced healthcare procedures. According to the
doctors who attended her birth, Louisa's outlook was
poor. My parents already had nine healthy children. Why
would they invest love and energy in their tenth, who
clung tenaciously to life despite all odds?

My mother described the moment she first saw Louisa, hours after the delivery which left Mom in critical condition. As the nurse carried the baby into the room, my mother's eyes met those of a little angel. Louisa's newborn gaze fixed on our mother across the room. Mom knew instinctively that this child was special. Not "disabled" or "challenged," but *special*. "What have I done to deserve such a precious gift?" was her immediate thought.

Louisa lived twenty-eight years. She was not successful by worldly standards. She was short and stocky, her complexion marred by cyanosis. She struggled in school, while her speech consisted of blunt, emphatic phrases. She never earned a cent, while her healthcare cost plenty. But Louisa loved life, with an unconditional, all-encompassing love. And her joy in life was contagious.

Plucky and adventurous, Louisa did not allow her disabilities to exclude her from family and class activities. She scaled mountains with the rest of us – on her brothers' backs, of course. And joining her class on a field trip to the sea, she rode triumphantly in a dune buggy constructed by friends, clicking her tongue and cheering the "horses" on as classmates took turns pulling her over the sand.

For Louisa, people were meant to be loved, occasions to be celebrated, and each moment savored to the full. Yes, life was an ongoing festival and each day provided opportunity to rejoice! She celebrated the birthdays and anniversaries of friends and family almost as much as her own – and *that* was something she anticipated for weeks in advance! Everyone in the family, as well as all her friends, received hand-drawn pictures for their birthdays each year. And when it came to weddings, she was an incurable romantic. When friends announced their engagement, Louisa donned princess attire and floated gracefully across the lawn to her favorite swing, where she proceeded to sing ballads while swinging happily, loose hair flowing and gown flapping in the breeze.

Through her last years, Louisa suffered increasingly because of her heart defect; yet she radiated peace. It was hard to see and hear her gasp for breath as her heart pumped more sluggishly. Her joints caused excruciating pain; she'd wince if I covered her with a light sheet. Infection set in at the end, and her systems shut down.

As she lay dying, she wanted music in her room. The Weavers and Beethoven's Ninth Symphony were her favorites, but any music was fine as long as it was upbeat. Our older siblings had children by this time, and often a baby slept quietly on Louisa's chest as she fanned her face for air. She lifted her stubby hand in a thumbs-up every time I entered her room, and she said repeatedly, "I'm for *life!*" On one of her final days Louisa told us, "My task is to bring *joy!*"

The Beatitudes say that the kingdom of heaven belongs to those who are poor in spirit and know their need for God. Louisa possessed these qualities naturally and radiated Christ unawares. She showed me how to live, through love that suffers and is kind (1 Cor. 13:4).

Jean Vanier, founder of L'Arche communities for the disabled, wrote in *Community and Growth,* "The poor are always prophetic. As true prophets always point out, they reveal God's design. That is why we should take time to listen to them. . . . That means staying near them, because they speak quietly and infrequently. . . . But if we listen to them, they will bring us back to the essential."

Modern society touts a different gospel: Blessed are you who achieve. Blessed are the prosperous, the politically successful, the powerful. Blessed are you who are beautiful and athletic. Blessed are those who win scholarships to prestigious universities.

Most of us strive for perfection. But what of people like Louisa? Why do they exist? Vulnerable and dependent, people with Down Syndrome are easily dismissed as "defective" and often aborted. And yet Louisa and the many like her are truly our teachers – for didn't Jesus admonish us to "change and become like little children"? I believe he charged us to welcome the Louisas of this world when he said, "Whoever receives this child in my name receives me. . . . For he who is least among you all is the one who is great" (Luke 9:48).

Dad

Those who have nothing have all, since they have God.

Evelyn Underhill

"WHO IS THIS GUY who comes into our house and tries to take over?"

Out of the house for years, my brother Henry had returned to help with our father's care; but with Alzheimer's disease, Dad no longer recognized his eldest son. As I prepared him for bed that evening, Dad appeared agitated and couldn't settle. "It seems to me I was annoyed with someone today," he mused. "Did I apologize to him yet?"

Amazed at his inner acuity despite advanced dementia, I reminded my father of the day's previous incident. "Shouldn't I apologize?" he asked, reaching for his robe and slippers. It was already late, but the two of us set off in search of Henry. Meeting him in the narrow hallway, Dad humbly asked his son's forgiveness for his earlier impatience.

My father, once a brilliant scholar and community organizer, suffered from Alzheimer's for fifteen long years. By the end, his brain was virtually destroyed; but he retained a fine sensitivity of soul – an almost heightened sense of how things should be, spiritually speaking.

Dad had always been wise and reliable. He raised us kids with strict discipline and – together with Mom – taught us to live intensely. His insight into world affairs, history, and the human condition was deep; people sought his advice. And with his dry humor and uncanny wit, Dad could be hilarious.

When younger, Dad was sometimes overbearing. He wanted things done right and insisted on near-perfection. He challenged anyone whose attitude seemed misguided and could be vehement in setting the record straight. Life was exciting with Dad, that's for sure.

As he neared seventy, Mom and I noticed a distressing new trend. Dad forgot to take his medications. And increasingly I found him searching for items he'd misplaced – which were usually right where he'd put them.

Puzzled and somewhat fearful, I spoke to Mom. Dad's father had died of Alzheimer's. Was Dad succumbing to that dread disease as well?

Because of her deep love for Dad, Mom instinctively compensated for his losses, recalling words when he groped mid-sentence and noting where he put things. But Mom died unexpectedly, and he began to flounder. I tried to fill her shoes, dispensing Dad's pills and keeping track of his belongings. I had the unenviable task of informing him that it was no longer safe for him to drive. I was afraid he would be angry; but instead, he thanked me. With tears in his eyes, he said, "I don't know what I would do without you."

There were hair-raising episodes that left me upset or Dad frustrated. One sunny fall afternoon, he appeared after his midday nap in his nightclothes. He put on his coat and started reaching for his hat and cane as I exclaimed, "Dad, you can't go out in your pajamas!" Without missing a beat he retorted, "Well, do you want me to go without them?" Out into the neighborhood he strode – in his fuzzy green PJs.

But Alzheimer's softened him. Formerly controlling, Dad now let others advise him. Graciously he turned over the steering wheel of life, allowing himself to be guided through the bewildering maze of dementia.

Granted, Dad struggled to let go of his independence and wept when he could no longer communicate coherently. But his surrender was dignified. Mellowed by the storms of life and chiseled by a lifetime of submission to God, he now spread a tranquility that drew people, especially kids. He sat on the back porch, smoking his pipe and watching the children play. He was happiest with me at his side, so we spent countless hours enjoying nature's beauties together.

Shortly before his death, I sat at Dad's side, his emaciated hand in mine. It smote my heart to see my father, previously so capable, lying helpless and unaware in a recliner. But a visiting friend handed me a quote from *Everyone Belongs to God,* by Christoph Friedrich Blumhardt, "God needs to have one of his children in every hell, because it is only *through them* that he can enter that hell in order to end it."

Could my father have been chosen to carry God's love into the hell of Alzheimer's? I'll never know in this life. But Alzheimer's humbled him, according him the poverty of spirit to which Jesus alludes in his opening Beatitude, "Blessed are the poor in spirit, for theirs is the kingdom of heaven."

2

Those Who Mourn

Blessed are they who mourn,
for they shall be comforted.

Heartbroken

Instead of explaining our suffering, God shares it.

Nicholas Wolterstorff

"**M**Y CURTIS IS DEAD. Heartbroken," read an email I opened on arrival at work one Monday morning.

I reread the terse message but couldn't grasp it – Curtis, healthy and in the prime of life, was – *dead?*

The email from Curtis's mother included no details, so I picked up the phone to call her. I've known Alberta and her husband Ray almost thirty years, since their daughter and I studied medical laboratory technology together at a local college. Entering my first lab seminar as an insecure seventeen-year-old, I was partnered with Sherri, an outgoing girl with an impish sense of humor. She joshed around about blood, pee, and poop, making it sound like they were old hat for her. Well, they sure weren't for me – yet! But my initiation was just around the corner.

"Each of you will now take a specimen cup from the table and bring back a urine sample to be examined by your laboratory partner," intoned our instructor. Sheepishly we made our way down the hall to the restrooms. Returning, embarrassed, to the classroom, Sherri handed me her specimen and I gave her mine. My urine was a clear pale yellow. But Sherri's was black.

Swallowing my shock, I sputtered, "Sherri, what's wrong with you?"

"I have sickle cell disease – but I'm gonna beat it!" Her reply conveyed fatigue as well as a determination I would soon come to associate with Sherri.

It didn't take us long to become friends. We laughed our way through hours of microscopy as we pursued the art of diagnosis. But weeks into the semester, Sherri collapsed. She was admitted to intensive care in critical condition and was fighting for her life.

Sherri suffered – a lot. It was distressing to hear her cry out and watch her struggle for breath. It was at her bedside that I first met her parents. After class each day, I'd head to the hospital to sit with her until they got off work. Her pain was mirrored in their eyes as they sat helpless by her side.

Over the next nine months I witnessed Sherri's agonizing decline until she died. She was twenty-two.

Heartache followed Ray and Alberta through the following years. Their youngest son Brian and his wife lost twin babies – a boy and a girl – and then had premature twins who survived, but just barely. One of them was diagnosed, like Sherri, with sickle cell disease. Worn down by years of sorrow, Alberta took on the appearance of a bronze relief etched with grief. Ray's sadness ran silent but deep, like water relentlessly carving canyons from rock.

Then came their son Curtis's unexpected death. No one was there when he died. When he'd failed to appear to preach to the kids at church that Sunday, a fellow pastor stopped by to inquire and found him dead on his apartment floor.

What do you say to a mother who suffers anguish as deep as Alberta's? And how do you comfort a father as he prepares to bury yet another child? I will never forget the sight of Alberta weeping, upheld by her husband as they followed their son's casket down the aisle.

On a visit shortly after Curtis's death, I asked Ray why he thought Jesus said those who mourn are blessed. Ray responded, "Our troubles and afflictions point us back to God. They lead us to a greater dependency on him. They humble us. Really, they're not given to us for ourselves per se but to help us do God's work."

"There's a scripture that says we're supposed to comfort others with the comfort we ourselves have received," he continued (2 Cor. 1:4). "I've experienced the reality of that. You can't teach something you don't really know. And you won't know unless you've been there. God uses our struggles to refine us – to show us things about ourselves we had no way of knowing before. And with that knowledge, we can comfort others."

An oft-sung chorus in Handel's *Messiah* declares, "Surely, he hath borne our grief and carried our sorrows" (Isa. 53:4). What a comfort it is to know that Jesus understands – and has borne – every sorrow we will know.

In his book *Lament for a Son,* Nicholas Wolterstorff takes us through the months that followed his twenty-three-year-old son's tragic death in a mountain climbing accident. His final reflection illustrates the transformative power of grief:

> If sympathy for the world's wounds is not enlarged by our anguish, if love for those around us is not expanded, if gratitude for what is good does not flame up, if insight is not deepened, . . . if aching for a new day is not intensified, if hope is weakened and faith diminished, if

from the experience of death comes nothing good, then death has won. So shall I struggle to live the reality of Christ's rising and death's dying. In my living, my son's dying will not be the last word. But as I rise up, I bear the wounds of his death. My rising does not remove them. They mark me.

Yearning

This is Christ's mission: to take the good news to the poor, to those who receive only bad news, to those who are always trampled by the powerful, to those who watch pass by, out of their reach, the riches that satisfy others.

Oscar Romero

"I FEEL LIKE I have work to do to come clean, but I don't know how to do it. Maybe it's too painful and I'm scared ..."

Sandy (not her real name) sat on my front porch, tears streaming down her face. It was a beautiful warm day; spring sun played over the grass while finches chirped in nearby trees. Nature seemed to cocoon us protectively as our conversation traversed Sandy's dysfunctional childhood. Having heard my own story from a friend,

Sandy had come over to talk. She was hurting badly but yearned for peace. That's not something I could give, so I simply listened:

I was born in Yonkers, to Italian parents. My grandmother died giving birth to my mother, so Mom was raised by an older sister who resented her existence every day of her life. Because of this, Mom never learned to show motherly affection to us kids. Desperate for the love she failed to give me, I cried out – and acted out. I lied and stole. I wished I'd get caught – anything to get attention – but that never happened.

My parents fought: there was screaming, yelling, and cursing. My father beat us with a belt. He loved to say that his kids would never amount to anything. If your apparent worthlessness is reinforced every day, you eventually start to believe it.

Dad kept a generous stash of porn magazines hidden in the basement. I found them. Flipping through, I began to obsess about my appearance as I compared myself to the models. It wasn't long before I was filled with self-loathing. One day, I took one of Dad's porn spreads to school and gave it to a boy. I was caught by the principal and shamed in front of the school. When I returned home that night, Dad met me at the door and beat me with a strap. I was covered in welts for days. Dad yelled, "You are not my daughter! No daughter of mine would do a thing like that!" I didn't dare tell him the picture came from his own magazine; that would only have evoked more wrath.

Dad taunted me about my appearance: first he mocked my hooked nose, then he said there was too much flesh on my hips. Later, I would seek out the services of a quack who botched both the nose job and an attempted liposuction. I suffered permanent damage from both. I never loved myself, because no one ever told me I was beautiful just the way I was.

Ignorant and misguided, I broke almost every commandment there is. Nobody cared. But believe it or not, I wanted to preserve my virginity. I must have picked that up at Catholic school. I tried; I fought off sex for a long time but eventually the guys wore me down. When you're fifteen and your mom lets you date a twenty-one-year-old man with a car, what do you expect? I was an insecure little girl trying to get love any way I could.

After that, there was no hope. Disgraced in my own eyes, I became promiscuous. I had abortions and got into drugs. I hung out with people who could have killed me. Deep down, I must have been looking for a way to end it all.

My dad died of a massive heart attack at the age of sixty-two; Mom's death followed five years later. So by twenty-eight I had lost both my parents.

Clinical depression set in for me, really deep. I met some nice guys who would have made good spouses; but, believing I was damaged goods, I turned them down and never married.

At the age of forty I found myself pregnant once again. I don't know why, but I prayed about this pregnancy. I was at a different place in life. I asked God, "Is this something you want from me, to be a mother to this child?" I woke with the certainty that I was supposed to have this baby.

Sandy's life was taking a turn for the better – or so she thought. This illusion was shattered months later when her son was born. Following her doctor's advice, Sandy had remained on antidepressants during the pregnancy. The drugs had adversely affected her child, who was born with physical and mental disabilities.

My son is a very special boy – and not just because he's mine. Since he was born I've realized that God's been pursuing me all along. He's given me this child whose purity and wisdom have been so healing to me. Caring for him gives me a wholeness I never had before.

In the Beatitudes, Jesus said that those who mourn are blessed. Could that include people like Sandy, whose lives are torn, jagged, and messy? She will readily admit that she is broken, debased by years of pain, sin, and abuse. Yet she yearns for what is pure and godly. Above all else, she longs to be free and whole. The psalmist declared, "The Lord is near to the brokenhearted and saves the crushed in spirit" (Ps. 34:18).

Jesus himself endured anguish and despair and understands every aspect of our humanity. In our darkest hours when we find ourselves floundering, he appeals, "Come to me, all who labor and are heavy laden, and I will give you rest" (Matt. 11:28–29).

3

The Meek

Blessed are the meek,
for they shall inherit the earth.

Luis

*God has two dwellings; one in heaven, and
the other in a meek and thankful heart.*

Izaak Walton

Scorching June sun radiated off the pavement
as I made my way toward a sprawling brick building
surrounded by concrete and blacktop. Sparse clumps of
grass between the sidewalk slabs were the only sign of
nature outside this institution. But a large sign cheer-
fully announced, "Welcome! Bienvenidos! William R.
Peck School."

Sister Jane Morrissey and I were on our way to meet
a student who attended Homework House, a free after-
school tutoring and mentoring program in Holyoke,
Massachusetts, run by the Sisters of St. Joseph. Entering

the boy's school, we were met by the vice principal, an optimistic man in his mid-to-late forties. The school hallways were bare, the cinderblock walls heavily scuffed. But a door soon opened to a host of bright-eyed faces, which lit with smiles on seeing Jane. "Sister!" the children called. Some waved happily; others came over for hugs.

Jane addressed every child by name. She asked one how school was going and inquired of another about last week's sports event and the siblings at home. "How are Mom and Grandma?" Jane asked a small girl who answered shyly, brown eyes asparkle under a mop of black hair accentuated by pink bobbles.

"We're here to meet with Luis," Jane informed the vice principal, who chuckled as he waved us toward the detention room. There sat Luis (not his real name) at a desk facing the wall, alone and embarrassed. Sister Jane commended him on being a leader – but reminded him to use his leadership skills for the good next time! At this, the detention monitor excused him, and the three of us set off toward the cafeteria.

Seated across a table from Luis, I looked into expressive dark eyes. He looked wise and weary beyond his years. "I'm ten," he began. "In fourth grade. My mom, my five sisters, and one brother – we live in a couple of rooms. Actually, one sister lives with my grandma because she couldn't take it no more at home. And one sister died when she was two minutes old."

"My mom uses the dining room as her room," he explained. "We can't go outside 'cause there's too many shootouts. In the old place we lived, there were lots and lots of shootouts and car crashes. There's lots of fights too. It's hard 'cause most of the time they are doing drugs and stuff." Luis's family is Puerto Rican. They live in a Spanish-speaking barrio where overcrowding and financial strain frequently erupt in violent clashes.

He's still a child, but he's obviously carrying responsibilities no child his age should have to bear. "I help my mom with the baby. Sometimes when it's raining and my mom's getting wet, I give her my sweater so she won't get sick, 'cause she gets sick quick. My mom can't work 'cause she has the baby, and if she would never have had the baby, she never would have worked 'cause she doesn't know how to read. I mean, she knows how to read, but she has to read it ten or nine times to herself so she can understand it."

Noticing a fresh zucchini I'd brought from my garden for Sister Jane, Luis got excited. "My mom loves squash! She eats it mostly every day. Yellow squash. She sometimes asks us, 'What do you want – rice and beans, or potatoes and squash?' I say, 'How 'bout we cook a feast?' and she goes, 'All right; we'll cook both of them!'"

"And your dad?" I hesitantly inquired.

Luis looked at the floor. "He's in Connecticut. We don't see him no more."

Turning our attention to Homework House, I asked how he likes the nuns' program.

"It's fun!" was his animated reply. "And there's *puzzles!*" His eyes lit up. "My mom says if we have no arguments this summer, she'll buy me some puzzles. They're gonna try to make me a big giant one for my birthday." From the way he talked, you would think he had just won the lottery.

True meekness is rare. Neither weak nor dispirited, the meek possess a strength of character unknown to people living in extravagance and ease. Luis is content with little; he enjoys small pleasures, finds satisfaction in helping others, and seems at peace about the things he cannot change.

Jesus tells us to garner imperishable treasures in heaven (Matt. 6:19–21). What are these treasures? The memory of Luis's face, glowing with pride and love for his mother, goes through my mind. Perhaps the "treasures in heaven" of which Jesus speaks are the seemingly insignificant deeds of love performed by the "least of these." Perhaps it is among the meek that the richest caches of heavenly treasures are found.

The Paradox of Meekness

I MET JO while volunteering as a chaplain at a hospice in southeastern England where she worked as a senior doctor for twenty years. Two decades of witnessing illness and death had not hardened her. Our paths crossed at the bedside of a woman who was obviously fatigued, her battle for life in its waning phase. Tears trickled down the patient's cheeks as she struggled to breathe. Jo crouched at her side to listen; their faces were level, their eyes communicating. Then, with an encouraging smile and a touch on the woman's arm, Jo rose to script an order to make her more comfortable. In a professional world of clipped heels and medical efficiency, Jo was a breath of fresh air.

Jo's a pantheist. She can be caustic about the failure of religion to respond to the immense suffering on our planet. Her expertise has taken her to many countries, teaching palliative medicine to doctors abroad. While modern advances have done much to alleviate suffering, Jo feels that we in the West are in danger of losing the human element in birth, illness, and death. And because of ethical dilemmas caused by regulations and technology's rapid advance, doctors are in danger of losing their joy in caring for patients. Jo points out that despite primitive technology and lack of funds, developing nations have done a far better job in providing emotional and spiritual support.

Jo does not romanticize poverty. She says, "An incredible amount of suffering exists in countries that lack access to drugs, surgical procedures, and sanitation. And yet people are supported." In Third-World cultures, she observes that God is still acknowledged as a living power in people's lives. Three years ago in Uganda she encountered a woman, paralyzed from the waist down and entirely dependent on others, whose smile lit the house where she lay dying. "It's because I have Jesus looking after me as well as the hospice," the woman confided. Then there was the young mother whose husband had died of AIDS, leaving her with three children to care for as she herself battled the disease. The destitute family lived in a mud hut; but, despite her circumstances, the woman felt upheld by a dream in which she had seen her husband, healthy and well-fed, in heaven.

I asked Jo how her experiences with the poor and dying connect with Jesus' words about meekness. "Reflecting on the Beatitude, 'blessed are the meek' in terms of my experiences in Africa, I initially thought of the many patients I've seen who are sustained by their faith and accept their illness as God's will – 'meek' being a reflection of patience and humility. But then I thought that this patience and humility are part of the problem; this attitude perpetuates continued suffering. I return from Africa both humbled and frustrated by people's meekness. Humbled by the three things they have in abundance that we have lost – faith, family, community – and frustrated by the poverty perpetuated by a corrupt system and the helplessness it engenders. Humbled too by how they get on with their lives and seem happier than we in the West who have so much but at the same time so little."

For many people, meekness implies passive submission, impotence, perhaps even spinelessness. However, Jesus exemplified meekness. Like the poor among whom Jo has worked, he submitted to suffering. Worldly rulers use force, but he promoted a kingdom in which "whoever would be great among you must be your servant, and whoever would be first among you must be your slave, even as the Son of Man came not to be served but to serve" (Matt. 20:26–28).

From Stable to Cross

Christ came for sinners – not for saints – and the way to
Christ is humility and poverty of spirit.

J. Heinrich Arnold

THE BITING COLD seemed particularly bitter as my
family made our way to the Christmas Eve service the
winter I turned eight. This was always the holiest night of
the year. When our pastor, Heinrich, told the Christmas
story, it seemed as if we too were on the arid hillsides
guarding sheep. This year again a live nativity – complete
with a donkey, some dirty sheep, and the pungent scent
of manure – drove home the poverty into which Jesus
had been born. The scene was warmed by candlelight,
radiating peace to all.

But I wasn't peaceful. Earlier that evening I'd gone to
feed my pet rabbit, Muffin, and found him dead.

"There was no place for him to lay his head." With his heavy German accent, Heinrich spoke slowly, each word drawn out with feeling. "Now, children, think of that. The great king of heaven and earth was born in a stable and had nowhere to lay his head."

I knew the story by heart, but it had never made me cry before. Heinrich continued, "Imagine the hardness of people's hearts, to reject God's son. But God sent him out of love, to bring hope and redemption to all. That is why the angels sang, 'Glory to God in the highest, and on earth peace, goodwill to men.'" The way he spoke, I could almost hear and see the multitude of the heavenly host.

The service concluded, we children followed our parents to greet Heinrich. He was so tall I had to tilt my head back to see his eyes, which looked keenly into my own. Turning to my mother, he asked about my tears; she explained about Muffin. Heinrich leaned down to me. "Now *that* is hard for a child to bear on Christmas Eve!" His eyes and tone told me he understood how badly it hurt. He cared! This encounter gave me a glimpse into the heart of God who regards the insignificant sparrow – and it comforted my grief; the wind didn't feel quite so cold on our walk home.

Heinrich loved people, and he loved Jesus. And because he himself had been schooled in suffering – as recounted in the biography *Homage to a Broken Man* – he understood the human soul. Deflecting flattery, he humbly listened to all who confided in him. He was drawn to the most broken, for in them he saw the bruised reed that God will not break, the smoldering wick he will not quench (Isa. 42:3). Whether it was a veteran tormented by flashbacks of Vietnam or a teenager fleeing the occult, Heinrich counseled patiently yet firmly, pointing always to Jesus, whose life began in a dirty stable and ended in execution alongside two criminals.

Through his surrender to God, Heinrich reflected Jesus' example of meekness. As he once said:

> We have nothing to hold to except the crucified Christ. We must ask ourselves again and again: Are we willing to go his way, from the stable to the cross? As disciples we are not promised comfortable and good times. Jesus says we must deny ourselves and suffer with him and for him. That is the only way to follow him, but behind it lies the glory of life – the glowing love of God, which is so much greater than our hearts and our lives.

4

Those Who Hunger

Blessed are they who hunger and thirst for righteousness, for they shall be satisfied.

Hunger for God on the Streets

It is not the one who has attained righteousness but the one who hungers for it whom the Beatitudes assert God blesses.

Bonnie B. Thurston

"SHE'S BEEN HUSTLING for twenty-five years, drinking and using heroin every night to drown her pain. But when she's out begging, she prays for everyone who passes."

I was listening to Laura Heffernan, a street chaplain with the London City Mission. She goes into hostels, brothels, and massage parlors to bring the gospel's hope-filled message to women on the margins of society. Laura and I had been introduced by a mutual friend.

"I've just come from the homeless hostel where I meet with a drug addict and alcoholic who suffers from huge amounts of shame," Laura confided. "It's ugly when she's strung out. But I meet her every week, to read from the Bible and pray. There's an imperceptible change slowly taking place. She used to leave the hostel only to beg or prostitute herself, but now she's coming out to church."

Laura described this woman's fall from prosperity to squalor. Coming from a wealthy background, she had entangled herself with a drug-dealing boyfriend. When he was caught, she was implicated and arrested. On her release from jail, her desperate circumstances led her into prostitution. Barely recognizable and deeply shamed after years of heroin addiction, she believes she's going to hell. Yet she yearns for wholeness.

I asked for Laura's thoughts on the fourth Beatitude, in which Jesus calls blessed those who hunger and thirst for righteousness. Her response was immediate. "It is those who are cast out by society as failures but who, knowing they are powerless, trust God in a way most of us don't. On the streets of London I've met women who are really, really hungry for healing. You don't often see a spiritual hunger such as I have encountered in these women."

According to Laura, these women ache for restoration the way a starving person craves food. By contrast, how many successful folk are satiated and overindulged? How many of us cry out daily for God? Do we thirst for spiritual nourishment, for the living water that wells up to eternal life (John 4:14)? If we examine ourselves honestly, we may discover that we are the people whom Jesus condemns as "having the outward appearance of righteousness but full of hypocrisy and lawlessness within" (Matt. 23:27–28).

Laura feels frustrated if Christians talk lightly about "transformation" as something easy to attain – with no understanding for people who feel trapped in a cycle of despair. "For us street chaplains," she says, "being a Christian means simply walking alongside the most broken of people day by day."

Jesus says that "many who are first will be last, and the last first" (Matt. 19:30), and that the prostitutes who have been written off by society will be welcomed into his kingdom first of all (Matt. 21:31).

Thirsty for Justice

Blessed are those who feel this hunger and thirst for justice, for the justice of the heart, of love, for the establishment of peace in unity. For they are the people who carry the pain of the world on their hearts, who carry the suffering of the world in their innermost being.

Eberhard Arnold

THE FIRST THING I SAW, as the elevator door slid open, was a gurney being whisked toward a door marked "Operating Room: Authorized Personnel Only." The patient looked like a young Hispanic man, from my brief glimpse. "God, another gunshot wound," Tom Rowan muttered as we stepped from the elevator and started down the hall. Turning a corner, we entered his office. I would have expected the chaplain of a busy Bronx hospital to have more real estate than the closet from which Tom performed his duties at St. Barnabas, but at least there were two chairs – and a door to shut out the corridor's chaos.

Having received several intriguing emails from Tom, I'd made an appointment to chat with him. On our way toward the bank of elevators, he was greeted by everyone we met, from security personnel at surveillance screens to housekeeping staff pushing carts of sanitizing agents.

Arriving at his office, Tom began to relate his life experiences. Raised in a Catholic family on Staten Island, he'd had a troubled childhood. His dad had been World War II infantry and returned with deep emotional wounds. Suffering from post-traumatic stress, Tom's dad found work with the Port Authority, painting bridges in the warm months and cleaning vents in the New Holland Tunnel in winter. Tom recalls, "Dad would tell me that he used to walk up on top of the bridges without any restraints or ropes. Some of the other veterans who worked with him would wait until a barge came by and then jump on it to commit suicide."

Being the eldest of four, Tom absorbed the brunt of his dad's pain: "When I did normal boyhood stuff, he beat me really severely. I never understood why." In an effort to escape his troubles, Tom started running. He remembers a coach saying, "To be a good runner, you have to run through your pain." But Tom's pain wasn't physical; it was the pain of having a father who could provide for his children materially but could not give them love.

Tom came of age during the Vietnam War. Attending Catholic high school from 1965 to 1969, he expected to find antiwar sentiment among his teachers. He was dismayed to see one after another leave for Vietnam. The military hype began to get to him. "Every night on the news America would say, 'Yeah, look; our body count is more than their body count.'" Because his father was emotionally absent, Tom's role models became people like the two Kennedy brothers, who were both assassinated. He began to wonder what was wrong with a country that killed off their best people.

Tom earned a degree in psychology but, unable to find employment, he returned to school for a degree in education of the blind. He married and took a job in his new field. But world events changed the course of his life.

On December 2, 1980, during the civil war in El Salvador, four Catholic missionaries from the United States were brutally raped and murdered there by members of the Salvadoran National Guard. News of this atrocity compelled the Rowans to re-examine their lives. "We had a house, we had two cars, and we lived in a decent neighborhood. My wife and I said to each other, 'Is this it? Is this all we're going to do?'" They applied to the Maryknoll Missionaries to go overseas as lay missioners with their two young sons. The family moved to Sao Paulo, Brazil, where Tom first taught literacy and later began ministering to victims of the widespread AIDS epidemic.

Because of his own difficult childhood, he could relate to the young men he taught in Brazil. He remembers asking why none of them had learned to read and write when they were kids, to which one replied, "We were children of farm hands, and there were no schools." The boy went on to describe the kind of treatment they had received as children. Tom recounts, "He was living on a sugar plantation, and he misbehaved. The plantation boss tied him to a pole and lashed his back, then filled a tub with salt water and immersed him in it."

Tom was influenced by Daniel and Philip Berrigan and drawn to the liberation theology preached by Oscar Romero and others in Latin America. These were voices that addressed the injustice and suffering he witnessed.

Through his AIDS work, Tom realized the importance of supporting people who are sick and dying. Returning to the United States after six years, he decided to become a chaplain, a vocation he continues today.

Those Who Hunger

All his life, Tom has been searching for peace, for a world where justice and love are real. His difficult childhood gave him an aversion to all forms of violence, hatred, judgment, and vengeance. "Hungering and thirsting for righteousness compels me to work to create right relationships – first with my God, next with myself, and then with others and all creation," he reflects. "There are many moments of satisfaction. The grace of this Beatitude is that it continues to challenge me to grow and change as I hunger and thirst for righteousness."

Ads bombard us daily with innovations to gratify our every desire, and many of us try to satisfy our hunger with material things, easy living, and the accolades of society. But Jesus refers to a hunger that cannot be satisfied by affluence, and he offers a deeper fulfillment to those who thirst.

The hurting and downtrodden still wait with open hands, longing for their thirst to be quenched. We may carry childhood pain and disappointment throughout our lives, but we can make of them vessels for the living water Jesus offers.

A Quest

It is the desire for God which is the most fundamental
appetite of all, and it is an appetite we can never eliminate.

Simon Tugwell

It was 1945, and my father, Richard Earl Domer,
had just returned from two years on an armed US Navy
freighter in the Pacific. The war had changed him,
permanently. Enlisting as an eighteen-year-old eager to
stamp out fascism, Dad had been posted as night mess-
boy in a tent hospital on Saipan. But he soon began to
question the validity of war.

> I had time on my hands and used it to read. It was there
> I encountered the writings of revolutionaries Henry
> Thoreau and Albert Schweitzer, whose thoughts opened
> my eyes, compelling me to reconsider my whole life.

During the long, beautiful tropical moonlit nights I
turned to God in prayer, seeking direction for my future.

Dad was on Tinian Island when the USS *Indianapolis*
came into harbor bearing the atomic bombs that were
dropped days later on the Japanese cities of Hiroshima
and Nagasaki. He was devastated. Such incomprehen-
sible loss of life. And to what end?

Enrolling at Manchester College in Indiana on
his return, Dad embarked on an intense inner search
inspired by Thoreau's observation, in *Walden,* that
"there are a thousand hacking at the branches of evil
to one who strikes at the root." What was the root of
evil, my father pondered, and how does one strike at
it? Perhaps he could somehow fight economic injustice;
wouldn't that strike at the root of evil? But a further
challenge from Thoreau convinced him he would have
to revise his own lifestyle to one that negated the causes
of poverty: "It may be that he who bestows the largest
amount of money on the needy is doing the most by his
mode of life to produce that misery which he strives in
vain to relieve."

Dad was convicted. Rejecting the American Dream
as an exploitative lie, he was determined to pursue
Schweitzer's insight that "the only ones among you who

will be really happy are those who have sought and found how to serve."

It was at Manchester that Dad met my mother, Lois Ann, an energetic, outgoing sophomore studying to become a school teacher. She had a beautiful soprano voice, and he first noticed her on a college choir tour. On breaks between performances the guys – and Mom – played ball. As my father watched her catching fly balls, he was smitten!

Deeply impressed by Dad's views on life, my mother joined him in his search. Like him, she was fed up with the capitalist mentality of every man for himself. They were married at a simple evening service in a rural Indiana church on June 18, 1948. They composed their own vows based on words in the biblical story of Ruth: "Where you go I will go, and where you lodge I will lodge; your people shall be my people, and your God my God; where you die I will die, and there will I be buried" (Ruth 1:16–17).

Drawn to a shared life "where no one has luxury until all have the necessities of life," they were soon branded communists. Disregarding McCarthy-era hype, Mom told her history classes that Russians were people just like everyone else. Her students liked her. They'd bring her fruit in season – and they kept her abreast of local rumors and gossip. Their reporting must have gone both ways, because it wasn't long before she was called before the American Legion – a veterans' organization that had no legal authority but a lot of clout after the war, particularly in the Midwest. When Mom got wind of their plan to question her, with a view to getting her fired, she talked with the school principal. He must have been a courageous man, because he told her to ignore the summons and said he would take care of it. He did. She kept her job.

Influenced by peace activist Garry Davis, Dad and Mom wondered about becoming "world citizens." They wrote to the State Department in Washington, DC, but were informed that the only way to formally renounce United States citizenship would be to leave the country. Their minds full of questions, they embarked on a year-long tour of Europe; perhaps they would discover the "brotherhood of man" rising phoenix-like from the ruins of the war. They took three-speed bicycles and raincoats that snapped together to form a tent.

Their quest took them to Albert Schweitzer's home in Gunsbach, France; his mandate to serve the poor and revere all life had been an ongoing inspiration. Although he did not know my parents were coming, Schweitzer gladly welcomed them in to talk and to spend the night.

During their hours of discussion, he encouraged Mom and Dad to continue their search for a practical way to live out their convictions.

On return from Europe, my parents joined Celo Community, an idealistic, social-minded cooperative in Appalachia, where Dad built a log cabin. Rejecting the use of animal products and living as simply as possible, they combined Schweitzer's reverence for life with Thoreau's directive to "simplify, simplify, simplify." From Celo, Mom wrote to her mother:

> All of nature here is so beautiful, it makes one have an attitude of worship. We feel that the most important thing for us now is to develop our inner, spiritual life. We feel certain that we will be led by God into the place where our lives will count the most.

While at Celo, my parents met representatives from the Bruderhof, a pacifist Christian community. Although disillusioned by organized religion, Dad and Mom were immediately drawn to – and eventually joined – these simple folk who not only preached Christ but tried to live his love every day. Mom wrote:

> We can never stop praising God for leading us to this life wherein we dedicate ourselves and all we have to him. I know of no other organization which is giving

as complete an answer of peace as this one. At last we know we are doing God's will.

In the fourth Beatitude, Jesus called blessed those who hunger and thirst for right to prevail. My parents, like countless others through history, hungered for justice – for peace and equity for all. They made their mistakes but continued to work for – and live out – true comradeship until the end of their lives. As my father reflected in his later years, "The way never changes, and Christ can always be found anew and fresh if we seek him constantly."

5

The Merciful

Blessed are the merciful,
for they shall obtain mercy.

Wielding Mercy

The Lord's mercy often rides to the door of our heart upon the black horse of affliction.

Charles Haddon Spurgeon

WHAT IS MERCY? Mercy means showing compassion to someone who is suffering, even when we could avoid it. It means pardoning when retaliation might seem justified.

My friend Elaine Roberts forgave under extreme circumstances, the likes of which most of us will never encounter. Her parents came from Jamaica, but she was born in England. She leaned toward atheism in her youth, but a series of life-changing events led her to faith. Three years after her wedding, Elaine learned she was expecting twins. However, eighteen weeks into the pregnancy there were complications, and both babies died. Although it left her heartbroken, this experience planted a seed in her heart; through her children, she had sensed the reality of a Creator.

Further tragedies followed. Shortly after the loss of the twins, Elaine's mother was held at knifepoint by a burglar and narrowly escaped with her life. A year later, a twenty-eight-year-old cousin was viciously hacked to death. And just two years after that, Elaine's world was again shattered. An early morning phone call on August 21, 1987, brought news that neighborhood youth, out for a lark the previous evening, had dragged logs onto the bike path her father regularly traveled. Returning home late at night, he was thrown off his bicycle and landed on his head; he fractured his skull and died.

Elaine was filled with a vengeance so fierce that her only desire was to trace her father's killers and annihilate them with her own hands. And as well as dealing with her own grief and rage, she now had to call her mother with the tragic news and accompany her to the morgue to make the identification. Elaine had never seen a dead body before. How could she bear the sight of her father lying lifeless and broken? She railed at God, "If you are real, prove it! And prove it to me now!"

"The next thing that happened was one of the most powerful encounters I have ever had with the living

God," Elaine recounts. "As I walked through the door into the room where my father lay, I felt what I can only describe as the most incredible warmth wash over my body. An unimaginable peace invaded my soul, and perfect love filled my heart for those who had killed my dad. Amazed, I heard myself say, 'It is OK.' From that moment, I have never been angry with the young men whose recklessness killed my father."

For most of us, being merciful is difficult; forgiving costs an inner battle. Our decision to forgive may have to be made repeatedly – perhaps daily – before we are entirely free from bitterness. Elaine attests that she could never have forgiven her father's killers on her own. She says the peace she experienced came as an unexpected gift and adds, "I began to understand that God deals with us according to his mercy, not as we truly deserve. And when I extend mercy to others, I treat them as God has treated me."

Chiseled

The key to becoming a merciful person
is to become a broken person.

John Piper

AN EARLY CHRISTIAN PARABLE compares
God's kingdom to the building of a marble tower whose
perfection requires every stone to be chiseled and fitted
by the stonemason. Like these stones, we must allow life
to shape us in painful ways. Kelvin Burke, a healthcare
chaplain on the Isle of Wight, experienced this dramati-
cally. He told me his story:

> At twenty-three it looked like I had it all going for me. I
> was sporty, flirty, and had a good job as an accountant. I
> played hockey in the Premier League and had an outside
> chance of being selected for Great Britain for the 1980

Olympics. I owned a four-bedroom detached house and was a practicing Christian. What more could I have wished? Then, on May 30, 1979, the bottom fell out of my rosy world.

I was on a church week away, hiking in the beautiful British Lake District. I and some buddies had just climbed Buttermere Fell with its spectacular views over Lake Buttermere, Honister Pass, and the famous Honister Slate Mines. We hiked back via Derwent Fell, pausing to enjoy the vista of mountains and valleys.

Returning to our campsite a short time later, we were nearing the top of Honister Pass when our car stalled, sped backwards, and crashed over the side of the mountain pass, falling into the ravine below. I was thrown out of the car and landed with the car pinning me face down in a stream with a complete spinal cord fracture at the level of the eleventh thoracic vertebra. My lungs were pierced, and I was paralyzed from the waist down.

As I lay there waiting for the ambulance, I heard the words of the Lord clearly in my heart, "I am with you always." This verse went through my mind repeatedly as I battled for life in intensive care.

Returning to work as an accountant, in full-length calipers after ten months in hospital, I was no longer the cocky youngster who set off to the Lake District the previous year. I now saw the needs of people around me. One was alcoholic; another had cancer. One guy was estranged from his wife, while the next was rich but lonely.

As I prayed and read in the Bible, I felt challenged to give up my business and become a full-time pastor. Not only had the accident paralyzed me for life, it had changed me spiritually.

Kelvin now serves as lead chaplain for the Isle of Wight NHS Trust, serving patients in both hospital and hospice.

Pastoral and spiritual work in a healthcare setting is intense. I encounter people seeking meaning and purpose. Assumed "givens" – independence, mobility, and good health – are stripped away, and life looks different following illness or trauma. Then along comes the chaplain in a wheelchair. And, because that twenty-three-year-old was trapped under a car off Honister Pass – broken and traumatized – he finds immediate rapport.

Kelvin has been deeply influenced by Henri Nouwen's concept of the "wounded healer," depicting Christ's brokenness as our way to new life. The wounded healer offers not ideology but himself.

The Beatitudes are interconnected. Poverty of spirit – whether inherent at birth or acquired through life's blows – makes us instruments of mercy. If we allow ourselves to be humbled by God for his purposes, we may become, in Mother Teresa's words, "pencils in the hand of a writing God, who is sending a love letter to the world."

Done for Him

Our mercy to each other comes from God's mercy to us.

John Piper

AWARE OF MY INTERESTS, a friend forwarded me a *New Yorker* article about a hospice nurse, Heather Meyerend. Intrigued by Heather's philosophy of "caring for the whole person, body and mind," I looked her up. A few weeks later, she visited. As we sat in the shade outside my home that hot summer day, she recounted the journey from her native Jamaica to Brooklyn, where her mother began working when Heather was in high school.

"I was directed to nursing through a particular verse in the King James Version of the Bible: 'But we were gentle among you, even as a nurse cherisheth her children'" (Thess. 2:7). At the time Heather had been preparing for a career in teaching, but she says, "My sense of following the Lord was like being carried in a current."

Her training complete, Heather found employment as a nurse. Disillusioned by the constraints of hospital nursing, however, she was soon drawn to hospice work. "With hospice, I felt I was making a profound difference. People embrace your presence in their lives because they are facing the end and are eager to have someone come along the way with them. Instead of jumping from one patient to the next, as in the hospital, I could now journey with one patient until the end." She shared some poignant stories.

"Sometimes you are there just to grant a simple wish," Heather says. She described her initial visit to the home of a new patient. Reaching out his hand, the man said, "Nurse, I would more than anything like to have a bath; I need to be washed!" Bathing was not Heather's responsibility as a registered nurse. "I could easily have said, 'The health aide will do that for you tomorrow morning,' but instead I said, 'No problem – I'll do that for you!' I washed him head to toe. He was so thankful; it was as if I'd given him a million dollars. His wife said, 'I've never seen such a bed bath!' It did something to me too. When I finished, I said, 'Wow, he looks good!' I had changed his clothes, combed his hair, given him clean sheets, and made him look nice. And would you believe it, he died the next day. It turned out to be a final sendoff."

Heather recalled a memorable encounter in Queens. "On one of my visits, the patient began discussing funeral plans. She made it clear she did not want her daughter to attend. I said, 'What do you mean, you don't want your daughter to attend? She's your daughter!' The lady replied, 'I haven't spoken to her in years!' I challenged her, 'You are facing death, and you have this unforgiveness in your heart?' My patient was Catholic, so I said, 'Listen to the Bible.' I opened to the Lord's Prayer and said, 'Let's look at this together.' At the passage where it says, 'Forgive us our trespasses as we forgive those who trespass against us,' I asked, 'Do you understand what that means? If we have received such forgiveness from God, how can we withhold forgiveness from others?' My patient listened, thank God; she decided to reach out to her daughter."

On Heather's next visit, the lady excitedly related that she had called her daughter to apologize, and they had reconciled. Heather sees helping a person let go of past hurts as an act of mercy. She continues, "At times we have to risk jumping into someone's life and saying, 'There are certain things you have to let go of – these things are like a chain tying you down.'"

A Scripture verse came to mind as I listened. It foretells the final judgment, when Jesus will welcome into his kingdom those who fed and clothed him and those who visited him when sick or incarcerated. Perplexed, the righteous will answer that they never saw the Lord hungry, naked, sick, or in prison – to which Jesus will reply, "Whatever you did for one of the least of these brothers and sisters of mine, you did for me" (Matt. 25:40).

6

The Pure in Heart

Blessed are the pure in heart,
for they shall see God.

To Trust as a Child

Whoever humbles himself like this child is the greatest in the kingdom of heaven.

Jesus of Nazareth

"JULIANNA WAS CLOSER TO JESUS than anyone I've ever met or known. It was obvious in her purity and love. She was almost always happy, in spite of intense suffering." I was listening to a mother who had just lost her five-year-old child.

In June 2016 a CNN headline had caught my eye. "Heaven over Hospital" told of a child's illness and death, yet the photos conveyed love and celebration – even fun and humor. The article described a little girl who enjoyed laughing with her brother, dressing like a princess, and dreaming up make-believe for her stuffed animals.

Julianna's story touched me. That's when I started phoning and corresponding with her mother, Michelle. In one communication, Michelle wrote, "The best way I can describe Julianna is to say that she was pure joy."

I was amazed that her mom could write of "pure joy," because Julianna had a hard life. Michelle – herself a neurologist – had consulted specialists about developmental delays she observed during her child's first year. She and her husband, Steve, were dismayed by the diagnosis, when Julianna was eighteen months old, of Charcot-Marie-Tooth Disease, an incurable neuromuscular disorder. As time passed, Julianna's parents and doctors realized with sinking hearts that the disease was affecting her breathing. Her life became a blur of respiratory emergencies and hospital stays.

The CNN feature reported: "By the time she was four, Julianna could no longer use her arms and legs. Her swallowing muscles were so weak she had to be fed through a tube in her stomach. Her breathing muscles suffered too, and she was in and out of the Doernbecher Children's Hospital in Portland, Oregon. But her mind worked perfectly."

Michelle and I first spoke just weeks after Julianna's death. She was grief-stricken. She was also struggling to accept the concept of God using suffering to achieve his purposes. She said, "My faith wasn't so strong that I could just trust. I battled to give up my control. But eventually I had no choice."

As Julianna steadily lost ground, her parents agonized to accept what the medical professionals were telling them: that continuing intervention was futile. They asked Julianna if she wanted to go to the hospital for more treatment or if she'd rather stay home, even if that meant she would go to heaven. That's when Julianna chose "heaven over hospital." Michelle says, "Julianna didn't worry. And everything changed for me when I started following her lead."

"Our conversations about heaven took my breath away," Michelle remembers. "Her answers were so fast and so clear. Julianna didn't want to go to the hospital again. At the age of four she chose heaven and told me not to worry because God would take care of her." Michelle says Julianna's simple trust "changed the way that *we* were looking at things; she showed us what was important to her and that she was not afraid."

Michelle attributes Julianna's serenity to her simple trust and ponders if this explains children's closeness to God. I am reminded of Jesus' reply to his disciples when they inquired which of them was greatest: "Unless you turn and become like children, you will never enter the kingdom of heaven" (Matt. 18:3–4).

It is children like Julianna – and those with childlike souls – who are truly pure in heart.

Purity in an Impure Culture

Who is pure of heart? Only those who have surrendered their hearts completely to Jesus that he may reign in them alone. Only those whose hearts are undefiled by their own evil – and by their own virtues too.

Dietrich Bonhoeffer

Is PURITY OF HEART outdated? Smartphones and iPads have hurled us into an age where the latest perversions are just one tap away. Anyone upholding biblical values is like a salmon swimming against the current, dismissed as out of touch in a society that gives free rein to every whim. But just as the salmon is drawn by an inborn compass to the waters of its origin, human beings too possess a hidden desire for what is pure and godly.

I first realized this as a young medical lab technician in a busy city hospital. The work was intense; we had a constant influx of specimens to process, while the phone rang off the hook with "stat" orders for urgent microscopic examinations of blood, bone marrow, and spinal fluid. Given that people's lives were dependent on the outcome of our analyses, the lab's atmosphere was charged. To ease the tension, my colleagues lapsed into a continuous flow of ribald jokes, irreverent suppositions about patients whose specimens we were examining, and explicit reviews of their own sexual experiences. Having chosen a life of chastity myself, working in this environment was challenging. Not wishing to be self-righteous, I simply focused on the work. Nonetheless, I felt like a fish squirming through oily mire in search of fresh water. Unnerved by my failure to join their banter, my colleagues wrote me off as a prude. But it wasn't long before they would stop mid-sentence, apologizing for their insensitivity. Tentatively at first, the tenor of our workplace changed until, by the time I left for a new assignment, the air was almost clear. I believe my companions were happier without the dirty talk – that inside, they too longed for cleanness.

God created the first man and woman "in his image" (Gen. 1:27), and he continues to create each person as a unique expression of his love. Life is a battle, though. Left to ourselves, we adults can never attain purity of heart. But before giving up, consider Jesus' words to his disciples who despaired at the impossibility of his demands: "With man this is impossible, but with God all things are possible" (Matt. 19:26).

Jesus came to pay our debt and restore us to righteousness. In fact, he never condemned but welcomed and spoke warmly with people whose sexual lives had been seriously derailed. Our part is to renounce "secret and shameful ways" (2 Cor. 4), embrace his redemptive offer, and allow our lives to be transformed. We must, in a word, repent.

Jesus' "Repent, for the kingdom of heaven is at hand" (Matt. 4:17) flies in the face of feel-good self-help therapies. But repentance is the road to restoration. In his book *Freedom from Sinful Thoughts,* J. Heinrich Arnold explains:

> Repentance does not mean self-torment. It may turn our lives upside down – in fact, it must – and at times we will feel as if the entire foundation has been swept away from under our lives. But even then we must not see everything as hopeless or black. God's judgment is God's goodness, and it cannot be separated from his mercy and compassion. Our goal must be to remove everything that is opposed to God from our hearts, so that he can cleanse us and bring us new life – that is, so he can fill us with Christ.

If we choose repentance, we will cry like King David:

> Create in me a pure heart, O God,
>   and renew a steadfast spirit within me. . . .
> Restore to me the joy of your salvation
>   and grant me a willing spirit, to sustain me.
> Then I will teach transgressors your ways,
>   so that sinners will turn back to you.
>
> (Ps. 51:10, 12–13)

Regardless of how far we have fallen, there is always hope. For, as the psalmist continues, "A broken and contrite heart you, God, will not despise" (Ps. 51:17).

And most encouraging of all: it is redeemed sinners who can love most fervently – forgiveness gives birth to love! A story in the Gospel of Luke powerfully demonstrates this connection. Invited to the home of a Pharisee, Jesus is visited by a sinful woman who anoints him with her tears of remorse while pouring expensive ointment over him. The Pharisees are indignant. Doesn't Jesus realize the woman's sinfulness? Jesus rebukes them, "I entered your house; you gave me no water for my feet, but [this woman] has wet my feet with her tears and wiped them with her hair. Therefore I tell you, her sins, which are many, are forgiven – for she loved much" (Luke 7:36–50).

Wholehearted Surrender

Purity prepares the soul for love,
and love confirms the soul in purity.

John Henry Newman

WHY WOULD ANY YOUNG WOMAN trade a
career as an Air Force flight nurse for a life of poverty,
chastity, and obedience?

Eileen Sullivan was born in Waterbury, Connecticut,
to devout Catholic parents. Entering nursing school as
America rolled through the turbulent sixties, she began
to drift away from her faith. When military recruiters
talked her into enlisting and she started her flight nurse
training, she felt she'd taken the first step into a life most
girls only dream of.

Eileen came close to marrying a physician. However,
the fact that he did not believe in God forced her to

reconsider – and rediscover – her own convictions. "I realized that I had to give my faith precedence. I knew I could
never commit my life to someone who did not share the
most vital part of me." She broke off the relationship.

Returning to Connecticut, Eileen worked as a cardiac
intensive care nurse for five years. She enjoyed the job, yet
part of her felt unfulfilled. She recalls, "I longed for love –
for a singular love." As further hopeful relationships did
not lead to the marriage she'd prayed for, she became
aware of a growing yearning. Slipping into the hospital
chapel during a night shift, she cried out in her heart,
"Lord, show me what you want me to do with my love!"

One cold January day, Eileen wandered into a
church as the priest was speaking about the millions
of unwanted children being aborted in our country,
urging the congregation to action. Something within her
responded to his challenge, and she began volunteering
at a crisis pregnancy center. Soon after, she and some of
the other volunteers attended a retreat. It was sponsored
by the Sisters of Life, a fledgling Catholic order.

Remembering that day as decisive, Eileen describes,
"Entering the room, I was met by the young postulants.
They had divested themselves of their professional
clothes and were dressed alike. They represented a spirit
quite opposite to the world where 'I gotta be me, I gotta

have my own signature and make my own mark on the world.'" One nun, Eileen learned, was a former IBM computer engineer; another had worked in robotics for NASA. "I said to myself, 'Wow! These women are happy – and it seems genuine.'"

It was their joy that drew Eileen to the sisters. Still, the following four years were tumultuous; she was only too aware that dedicating herself to God, as she felt drawn to do, would require her to renounce her career, as well as friends and family. "I had to do the leap of faith from 'A sister – me? Not even an inkling of a chance!' to 'Wow! Could this be an option?' to 'I need to really pray about this!' to 'I think He's inviting me.'"

Eventually coming to believe that her heart was made not just "for another" but "for many," she took the plunge. Donning a nun's outfit for the first time, Eileen – now Sister Veronica Mary – "was reminded of the scripture that entreats us to 'put on the new self, created after the likeness of God in true righteousness and holiness' (Eph. 4:24). Although it broke my heart to see my mother weeping, I felt such joy: 'God, now I can give my heart totally to you!'"

Even though she now wore a habit and veil – and believed that through her vows she was declaring Christ's victory over the forces of death that threaten our world – Sister Veronica's transformation was not finished. "I had to unlearn so many things. Moving from a human perspective to one focused on God took time and patience." But as she struggled to surrender herself entirely, she experienced more and more of the peace that had previously eluded her. Looking back on that time, she reflects, "All of a sudden you live, move, and breathe with this deep conviction that you are part of something greater than yourself."

Sister Veronica says that celibacy, too, required years of struggle. "There are going to be tensions throughout life in that area because we are made male and female. Our vow of chastity is a protection, but it's never a matter of renouncing your God-given nature as a woman. Coming in from our culture of today, it takes years to purify your mind, years to purify your heart. It is unrealistic to think that as soon as you enter the convent and put on this habit it's going to get easier. It can often be harder, because all of a sudden you realize, 'My life is not my own, and I'm committing to growing in holiness.' And that is not easy. Many days it is very difficult."

Like Sister Veronica, I have struggled with this issue. A close friend helped by telling me that purity does not consist solely in rejecting self but in offering God a wholehearted "yes!" in response to his love. Purity, therefore, is more than moral self-discipline; it is connected with single-minded devotion to God. I cannot serve him with one hand while grasping for the world with the other. As Jesus said, "You cannot serve two masters" (Matt. 6:24).

In a conversation with Brother Leo about purity of heart, Saint Francis advised him not to be preoccupied with his spiritual state but rather to focus on Christ. Looking to Jesus, Leo could forget himself and be free to love.

Purity, then, is perhaps not a matter of perfection but a matter of the inclination of our hearts.

7

The Peacemakers

Blessed are the peacemakers,
for they shall be called children of God.

Building Peace One
Person at a Time

*Those who bring reconciliation to broken relationships are
carrying on the work of Jesus, the Prince of Peace.*

George M. Dupree

HUMAN CIVILIZATION IS hardly a picture of
peace and harmony. Historians chronicle a never-ending
saga of empires battling to control territories, assets, and
peoples; the world's current state is no better.

While none of us individually can bring about peace
on an international scale, each of us can be a peacemaker.
Countless individuals work quietly for peace in their
homes and communities. Although rarely featured in
the media, ordinary people do make a difference. It only
takes a pebble to trigger an avalanche.

Take Robin Wildman, for example. A fifth grade teacher from a conservative Jewish background, she was unwittingly drawn into peacemaking when local law enforcement conducted a Community Works program at Broad Rock Middle School in Rhode Island.

In January 2001, a police captain brought Dr. Bernard LaFayette, one of Martin Luther King Jr.'s coworkers, to speak to Robin's class. Inspired by the experiences he shared, the children raised funds for a five-day tour of civil rights movement landmarks in the South. LaFayette returned to the school many times, impressed by the students' enthusiasm. He trained them, their parents, and their teacher in a nonviolent approach to resolving conflict.

In King's historic book, *Stride Toward Freedom,* written after the Montgomery bus boycott, he laid out six principles of nonviolence. After King's death, Lafayette compiled a training manual based on these ideas. Acknowledging its positive effect on her pupils, Robin decided to incorporate this training into her classroom curriculum.

Robin's dream is for all Rhode Island's students to be trained in nonviolence. Broad Rock serves as a model. What was formerly the school's detention hall is now called the Reconciliation Room. Staff volunteer their time as "peace coaches." Any student charged with misbehavior is assigned a peace coach who guides him or her through several steps to reconciliation. Students must acknowledge their errors and show that they are sorry; they must repair damaged relationships by seeking forgiveness and justice; and they must continue to work on nonviolence skills long-term under the vice principal's guidance. Last year the school had no repeat offenders.

To be true effectors of peace we must first be at peace in our own hearts. In my experience, this peace is won through battle. Every time we overcome the evil within us, seek forgiveness, or pardon those who have wronged us, our hearts are flooded with peace. This peace may be threatened repeatedly in the course of a single day. But if we patiently strive for it within ourselves and in our relationships, we can contribute to the realization of King's "beloved community."

Robin began by simply applying the principles of nonviolence to herself and her students. She then talked with her principal, who offered unconditional support. Inspired by their example, other schools have followed. Might this be a growing avalanche toward world peace, loosed by a single pebble?

A Small Peacemaker

He has made everything beautiful in its time. He has also
set eternity in the human heart. . . .

Ecclesiastes 3:11

PEACE IS OFTEN ASSOCIATED in our minds with
historical giants like Gandhi. But anyone can be a peacemaker – even a stillborn child.

When my friend Magda's third son was born, he
looked perfect – each tiny finger and toe. He resembled
his older brother Russell, Magda recalls, with a broad
chest and little muscles on his arms. He even had his
dad's dimple on his chin. But no life coursed through his
little body; his soul had already departed.

As the preceding months passed, Magda had been
thrilled how this pregnancy was progressing; early scans
showed her baby's organs developing normally and his

heart beating strongly. In growing expectancy, Magda began the countdown to his arrival in the New Year. But in early November she acknowledged, with a sense of foreboding, that for two weeks her baby had been unusually quiet in the womb – and the past few days there had been no movement at all. Her diary records:

> Mommy felt your last little kicks on Saturday evening, October 31. Our family had gathered to sing. Those last precious kicks you gave me, Benjamin, were a real farewell – a moment I'll never forget.

When her husband Ben drove her to the local hospital, scans confirmed what the mother instinctively knew; her baby had died. Ben and Magda turned to God in prayer. "We made a conscious decision to accept what was happening as part of God's greater plan," Ben recalls. "We chose to trust our heavenly Father. In acceptance, we found the peace that passes human understanding."

Still, the pain of grief was indescribable. Magda attests, "You're going to grieve even if you have peace. You wouldn't believe the intensity of the bond between a mother and her child. It is there from very, very early on – an incredibly deep bond."

When she went into labor, their church met to pray and sing, and the pastor's wife joined Ben at Magda's side. Handel's *Messiah* was playing softly in the delivery room. Just as Benjamin was born the recording proclaimed, "But thanks be to God, who giveth us the victory through our Lord Jesus Christ!" Magda says, "Remarkable as it may seem, that's really what we felt when Benjamin was born; even though it was intensely painful, his birth was, somehow, a victory."

Church members have told Magda that they were brought up short on hearing that her unborn baby had died. Engrossing activities and petty disagreements faded in comparison. Crying out against the loss of her son with every fiber of her being, Magda nonetheless realized that God's purpose for Benjamin was being fulfilled; he was bringing peace to many. As they rallied around Benjamin's family, the whole congregation was touched by his brief life.

Jesus says, "Peace I leave with you; my peace I give to you. Not as the world gives do I give to you. Let not your hearts be troubled, neither let them be afraid" (John 14:27). Each of us encounters situations that threaten our peace. For one it may be the loss of a child, spouse, or close friend. Another may have received a difficult diagnosis. The key lies in our response: will we resist, or will we embrace God's plan? For Magda, peace came only through the acceptance of God's working in her – and her baby's – life. She still mourns; it is never easy to relinquish our dreams. But God's ways are not our ways. In longing for her son, Magda's heart is drawn, as if by a magnet, to the day when all separation will be overcome.

There are few who have not experienced loss. But our sorrow is not in vain, for the souls of our loved ones bind us to eternity. And when, in stillness and silence, we draw near to God, we are enveloped in his peace.

At Peace with Terminal Illness

*Once our personalities are honestly entrusted to God,
we can be sure there is nothing in life or death that
can alter the fact that our lives are lived "in God."
That makes for a deep inner peace.*

J. B. Phillips

"How much time do we have?" Allen asked.

Looking intently at Allen's wife, Marcelle, the neurologist asked, "Do *you* want to know?"

She nodded.

The doctor replied, "You have months; not weeks, but months."

Allen and Marcelle had been visiting friends in Strasbourg, France, when she fell in their apartment. She laughed it off as a normal consequence of turning sixty-three; but there were subsequent falls – and increasing weakness severe enough for Allen to get Marcelle a wheelchair.

Realizing something was seriously wrong, they returned home to England for rigorous testing. Their doctor had called them in to review the results, and here was the distressing diagnosis: "You have amyotrophic lateral sclerosis." ALS, also known as motor neurone or Lou Gehrig's disease, attacks nerve cells controlling the muscles, resulting in increasing weakness and paralysis. The course that the disease takes varies, but it is always fatal.

Their trip to France had come to an abrupt end, but Allen and Marcelle sensed that God was assigning them a different task, which they desired to fulfill to the best of their ability. To the terrifying prospect of death from respiratory paralysis, Marcelle responded simply, "I am ready to go, if this is the time to go."

Life became painful as Marcelle lost the use of her limbs and the ability to speak. Eventually she could not so much as brush an annoying hair from her cheek, blow her nose, or change position. Able to communicate only with her eyes at the end, her active mind was locked in. Because it leaves the mind intact but trapped in a paralyzed body, late-stage ALS is one of the leading conditions used by "death with dignity" advocates to justify physician-assisted suicide. But Allen and Marcelle were not going that route. They believed that when God gives someone a cross to bear, he also gives what it takes to bear that cross – to the end. While she could still speak, Marcelle urged those around her to "accept God's will for your lives as it comes to you, as I want to do."

Always a gentle and unassuming person, Marcelle used her last vestiges of speech to express heartfelt thanks. Because of her attitude, a peaceful atmosphere surrounded her bedside, which became a gathering place. Neighborhood children came daily to greet her, and friends sat quietly by her side. God's presence was with her as she courageously journeyed toward the next life. Her parting gift was one of peace.

Having known Allen and Marcelle as family friends for over thirty years, I believe the peace that surrounded her final months resulted from a lifelong quest for God and obedience to his will. Marcelle was born in Morocco, a descendant of Jews who fled the Spanish Inquisition. She said, "Growing up as a Jew in an Arab country, it was ingrained in me not to fight but rather to work things out peacefully." Her father was respected by both Jews and Arabs as a peacemaker. He affirmed the source of his peace when tragedy struck. Marcelle's three-year-old sister fell from a neighbor's balcony and died two days later.

Marcelle never forgot her father's response, as he quoted, through his grief, "The Lord gave, and the Lord has taken away; blessed be the name of the Lord" (Job 1:21).

In Marcelle's early childhood, a missionary read Bible stories that deeply impressed her. Years later, as a teenager, she was invited to a Christian camp for Arab girls, even though she was Jewish. It was here that she became convinced that Jesus was the fulfillment of Old Testament prophesies. Marcelle remained true to this belief for the rest of her life. There were obstacles to face and battles to be won, but she repeatedly experienced that "since we have been made right in God's sight by faith, we have peace with God because of what Jesus Christ our Lord has done for us" (Rom. 5:1).

It was at a youth Bible study in Casablanca that she met Allen, a young serviceman stationed at an American navy base in Sidi Yahia. They married and began searching for a practical way to live out their faith. Moving to Spain, they formed a small community with like-minded couples at Naval Air Station Rota, where they continued their search. Allen and Marcelle eventually joined my community, the Bruderhof, and became enthusiastic participants in community life and outreach.

Allen describes Marcelle as "a woman of peace." When disagreements occurred, she was the first to look for reconciliation. Her steady love and deep faith served as an anchor for her nine children and for all who knew her.

Marcelle was truly at peace. Near the end of her life she witnessed, "It is God who is faithful, not us. He held me in his hands all this time. When I struggled, he always brought someone into my life who helped me at the right time. It was like God saying to me, 'I will never leave you alone.' And that is really what happened."

8

The Persecuted

Blessed are they who are persecuted
for the sake of righteousness,
for theirs is the kingdom of heaven.

Confronted by Truth

One wonders why Christians today get off so easily. . . .
What are the things we do that are worth persecuting?

Clarence Jordan

T HE THOUGHT of persecution for righteousness'
sake has always evoked mental images for me of early
Christian martyrs flung to the lions or Reformation-era
dissidents burned at the stake. While such persecution continues in today's world, it is mostly confined to
isolated totalitarian regimes and areas under threat of
ISIS militants. Granted, violence might erupt anywhere
these days, given the frequency of terrorist attacks, but
for most Westerners, such persecution remains remote.

There are, however, less obvious – and possibly more
insidious – forms of intolerance. Like many other

people in recent years, I have experienced opposition to my faith here in America, sometimes in the most unlikely places. After enrolling for religion courses at a Mennonite college in the Midwest, I was surprised to be taken to task for upholding a simple faith in Jesus as the Son of God and for believing in his miracles and the virgin birth; early in the semester, I found myself locked in debate with the department head over these tenets, which for me were nonnegotiable.

This experience was unpleasant and frustrating – but I was only taking classes, not earning my living. The situation had been more serious for Dr. Alice von Hildebrand, now retired, whom I recently visited at her home in New Rochelle, New York.

Fleeing Nazi occupation of her native Belgium in 1940, Alice arrived in America as a seventeen-year-old refugee. Inspired by a talk at the house of her future husband, philosopher and theologian Dietrich von Hildebrand, she pursued a master's degree in philosophy at Fordham University. She had difficulty finding employment to support herself while completing her PhD, however; although she was a devout Catholic, Catholic universities did not take women as philosophy professors back then. She was eventually employed at Hunter, a secular college in New York.

In her book *Memoirs of a Happy Failure* Alice recalls, "I had never taught in my life. Moreover, with my European background, which presumed respectful, receptive students, I knew I was ill-equipped to face assertive (and often arrogant) students who came from a totally secular background." Thus began a difficult thirty-seven-year career. In her memoir Alice writes, "I thank [God] for not having revealed to me how arduous my task would be: to hold high the flag in defense of the objectivity of truth in a fortress of relativism."

Alice told me she'd felt persecuted at Hunter from day one. She continued, "The word 'truth' is simply a challenge – because people know full well that if they admit there is an objective truth, they have to bow and obey!" In her memoirs she describes a student announcing in class, "The worst thing that could happen to me would be to find out that I have an immortal soul; then my actions would have consequences for me."

Because Hunter's philosophy department was largely staffed by secular humanists who emphasized the subjectivity of truth and wisdom, Alice found herself at loggerheads with colleagues who resented her insistence on one ultimate, universal truth, which, Alice maintained, was God. "I never spoke of faith in God or Christ," she told me. "But if someone finds the truth, he automatically finds God, because God *is* the truth. Jesus said, 'I am the truth.' He didn't say, 'I *have* it'; he said, 'I *am* it'!"

Barred from teaching day classes, where pay was good and benefits secure, Alice was relegated to evening sessions where she was paid by the classroom hour without medical coverage and received neither credit nor compensation for time spent counseling students. She was never promoted.

Despite the opposition, young people were drawn to Alice. She recalls, "When I taught, through much suffering and prayer, I was able to awaken in my students a longing for the truth." More than one came to faith, not through her words but through the love they encountered in her classroom. Her popularity was envied by fellow faculty; false rumors were spread – among them, that she was recruiting converts and that she was anti-Semitic. On her retirement in 1984, however, Hunter College gave her a special award – after the student body of 25,000 gave her the highest evaluation among the approximately 700 professors teaching there.

Alice is convinced that the years of animosity were a blessing: she was reminded daily of her dependence on God. "Persecution made me realize that without God's help I could not do it," she recounts. "Faith can only be received on your knees."

As she lives out her final years, Alice encourages others to embrace opposition. "Rejoice when you can't do it on your own," she says, "for when we turn to God for help, *joyfully* acknowledging defeat, we defeat the defeat!"

To understand the final Beatitude, we must reflect that while history recounts a succession of rulers who sought to conquer and control, Jesus said he was sent "to proclaim good news to the poor, to proclaim freedom for prisoners, recovery of sight for the blind, and to set the oppressed free" (Luke 4:18). It is little wonder that his kingdom posed a threat to the political and religious elite of his time. And he asks us to represent his counter-cultural kingdom in our day.

No Greater Love

You will be met with hatred because you bring justice,
and you will be persecuted and hounded to death for not
taking part in injustice. But you will be received with great
love in huts that are open for you, and you will be
taken in because you bring love.

Eberhard Arnold

 A NNE SCHWERNER WAS one of the spunkiest
people I've known. But there was a tenderness about her
too – a dimension I didn't fully comprehend as a child;
Anne had been deeply wounded, both by the brutal
murder of her son and because her faith in the goodness
of humanity had been broken.

It all began on a June night in Meridian, Mississippi.
Tensions were high in America during that summer of
1964, as more than a thousand volunteers – many of them

white college students from the North – responded to a plea from civil rights organizations to help register black voters in the South.

In January of that year, twenty-four-year-old Michael Schwerner had quit his job as a New York social worker; he and his wife Rita had decided to leave home and drive their VW Beetle 1,100 miles to Mississippi. Having participated in integration efforts in northern states for several years, Mickey was eager to work for justice and equality in the Deep South. The Congress of Racial Equality, a national civil rights group, tasked him with helping to establish a community center in Meridian.

Like his mother, Mickey loved people, especially the disenfranchised. His warmth and enthusiasm quickly won the trust of his new coworkers. But the same qualities – plus his determination and leadership skills – earned him the hatred of white supremacists.

Rita later testified, "In the first few weeks that Michael and I were in Meridian, we had to change our place of residence some three or four times, because the black families who took us in received intimidating phone calls and became afraid to house us. . . . As we achieved some success in establishing the community center, the threats and intimidation began to increase. By May we received so many phone calls at late hours of the night that in order to get some sleep we were forced to remove our telephone receiver before going to bed."

On June 21, Mickey and two other young civil rights workers – Mississippi native James Chaney and Andrew Goodman, who had arrived from New York the previous day – were murdered by members of the Ku Klux Klan, then secretly buried in a remote dam. As FBI agents conducted an extensive search for the missing three, the world's attention was drawn to the struggle.

In Pelham, a quiet suburb of New York City, Mickey's parents were stunned to receive news of their son's disappearance. Mickey's father, Nat, was a Columbia-trained lawyer working with the American Civil Liberties Union; his mother, Anne, taught high school biology. Secular Jews who had no use for organized religion, the Schwerners had always worked for the betterment of society. Their world was shattered on August 4, when the decaying remains of their son and his friends were unearthed near Philadelphia, Mississippi.

Flipping through the *New York Times* several days later, my father saw a photo of Carolyn Goodman weeping at Newark Airport as her son's body was removed from a plane. Dad was soon on his way to New York City with his friend Heinrich Arnold in the hope of extending sympathy and solidarity to the grieving parents. Finding the Goodmans away from home, the two moved on to the Schwerners' house and knocked at the door. Nat and Anne were understandably wary of strangers. My father recalled, "As Mrs. Schwerner came timidly to the door, Heinrich – a tall man – took off his hat and leaned down toward her, speaking with such humility and love that she invited us in."

Thus began a decades-long friendship. Three years after their son's death, Nat and Anne were invited by Heinrich to the wedding of his own son, Christoph, which led to further visits. Christoph and his wife, Verena, became youth leaders in our church when I was in my teens; they frequently invited the Schwerners to share their concerns and insights, challenging us young folk to expand our horizons – to become participants in the worldwide struggle for justice. These lively discussions helped shape my thinking and made a lasting impression.

In his final Beatitude, Jesus calls those who are persecuted for righteousness' sake blessed. The Schwerner family certainly exemplified righteousness. After their son's death, Nat and Anne declined public honors for him; they said the case had only gained national scrutiny because Mickey was white, while deaths of countless black people – beaten, lynched, or drowned – remained uninvestigated.

Another of Jesus' sayings comes to mind as I reflect on what it means to be persecuted for the sake of righteousness: "Greater love has no one than this: to lay down one's life for one's friends" (John 15:13). This love was demonstrated by three young men on a dirt road in backwoods Mississippi, and their witness stands as a challenge to this day.

He Was There

You have formed us for Yourself,
and our hearts are restless till they rest in You.

Augustine of Hippo

It was cramped and airless in the sparsely furnished apartment where I sat with Sister Chantal, superior of the Missionaries of Charity in West London, just days after four members of her order had been gunned down by Islamic State jihadists. Sister Chantal raised both hands as she lifted her eyes to heaven. "We have had no details of how it was. They were in Yemen, you know, and none of us can get into the country to claim the bodies or speak with the one sister who survived. We know she is safe, but she is in hiding."

On hearing of the killings at the Home for Aged and Disabled in Aden, Yemen, I'd made the two-hour trip to visit the London-based sisters of Mother Teresa's order. News coming out of Yemen is sketchy at best, but Sister Chantal told me what she knew.

While serving breakfast to their patients on Friday, March 4, 2016, Sisters Anselm, Marguerite, Reginette, and Judith were forcibly handcuffed by armed men who'd entered the care home under the pretext of visiting their mothers. The sisters were then shot in the head. Twelve other staff members were also killed as they tried to defend the nuns. The surviving fifth sister had hidden when she heard the shouting. A visiting priest from India had also disappeared, presumably abducted.

Sister Chantal continued, "The attack was a calculated ambush on the sisters. None of the eighty care-home residents were killed, just the sisters and the staff members who sought to protect them. The gunmen smashed all the crucifixes and religious symbols in the home." Sister Chantal became animated. "Because they gave their lives every day, the sisters were ready. And what is more, the love our sisters gave to the people in Yemen prompted twelve others to give their lives to defend them! Some of those were definitely not Christian – but they had witnessed the sisters' love in action. They died protecting that love."

The slain sisters were originally from India, Kenya, and Rwanda. Sister Chantal said that in 1998, after three others from the same order had been martyred in Yemen, their provincial superior met with the remaining nuns, offering reassignment to safer territory. Each of them, on her own, chose to stay. Who else would care for their elderly people? Yemen needed the light of Christ, and they were prepared to be that light.

"Our sisters could not have given their lives that day if they had not given them to Jesus *every* day, beforehand. The love of Jesus was working in secret all these years while our sisters quietly served. We don't see a child growing in his mother's womb; he grows hidden and silent. But then in God's time, through suffering, he is born into the light of day, to be seen by all." Sister Chantal went on, "People ask us what we are doing for the world. Apparently nothing! But our Lord says, 'I only ask that you give a living witness of love.'"

Sister Chantal's face lit up as she said, "In the eyes of God, we cannot see this as a loss. Humanly, perhaps, we have lost our sisters. But not even death can break the chain of love!"

Our conversation turned to Good Friday and Easter, the holy days soon approaching. Sister Chantal quietly recited a passage from the Gospel of John: "Having loved his own who were in the world, he loved them to the end" (John 13:1).

"To the end," she emphasized. "God always asks for a total commitment. His commitment to us was total. And so must ours be." She expressed her grief that none of their community had been at their sisters' side in their final hour. Then she added simply, "But *He* was there."

Postscript

IN AN INCREASINGLY SECULAR WORLD, many people dismiss Jesus' Beatitudes as inapplicable. Indeed, his words fly in the face of upward mobility.

It would be convenient if we could brush the Beatitudes aside as an outdated code of conduct – or a recipe for sainthood meant for a select few. But I believe Jesus' words to be a timeless guide. Throughout the Gospels he urges us to be transformed – not by climbing the ladder of success but by allowing our own greatness to be stripped away.

Some translations of the Beatitudes use the words, "Happy are those . . ." instead of "Blessed are . . ." In fact, the term beatitude comes from the Latin *beātitūdō,* meaning "happiness." What is lasting happiness, and how is it attained?

Society promotes technological advancement and financial security. Commendable and desirable as these are, even better is Christ's promise of peace – not as the world offers, but true peace of heart.

In these pages you have met some of the happiest people I've known. They were not spared suffering but, through it, were transformed.

As we each continue along our way in life, let us heed the guides God sends to cross our paths. They may appear crippled or hungry. We may encounter them in a detox unit or prison cell. They may speak to us through the eyes of the dying or the cry of the bereaved. But through them we begin to view the world through Jesus' eyes, discovering the truths he taught us:

Blessed are the poor in spirit, for theirs is the kingdom of heaven.
Blessed are those who mourn, for they shall be comforted.
Blessed are the meek, for they shall inherit the earth.
Blessed are those who hunger and thirst for righteousness, for they shall be satisfied.
Blessed are the merciful, for they shall obtain mercy.
Blessed are the pure in heart, for they shall see God.
Blessed are the peacemakers, for they shall be called sons of God.

Broken but Blessed

Blessed are those who are persecuted for righteousness' sake, for theirs is the kingdom of heaven.

Related Titles from Plough

Be Not Afraid
Overcoming the Fear of Death
Johann Christoph Arnold

Seeking Peace
Notes and Conversations Along the Way
Johann Christoph Arnold

Cries from the Heart
Stories of Struggle and Hope
Johann Christoph Arnold

Escape Routes
For People Who Feel Trapped in Life's Hells
Johann Christoph Arnold

Freedom From Sinful Thoughts
J. Heinrich Arnold

Plough Publishing House
1-800-521-8011 ◆ 845-572-3455
PO BOX 398 ◆ Walden, NY 12586 ◆ USA
Brightling Rd ◆ Robertsbridge ◆ East Sussex TN32 5DR ◆ UK
4188 Gwydir Highway ◆ Elsmore, NSW 2360 ◆ Australia
www.plough.com

Want to give this book to a friend? And keep it too? Now you can: if you pass this book on, we're happy to replace it for free. For details visit *plough.com/give*.

CPSIA information can be obtained
at www.ICGtesting.com
Printed in the USA
FFOW03n1104080618
47046235-49361FF